A Study in
Romans

D.R. Olson

Copyright ©2021 by Douglas Robert Olson
All rights reserved.
ISBN: 978-1-7358126-1-8

Preface

This book consists mainly of questions. I hope to help the reader learn truth as he turns to the Holy Bible to answer them.

I have used several kinds of bullets throughout the book. The symbol • introduces a question or a paragraph that contains a question and the symbol ○ introduces a list of references to verses that relate to a question. The reader can record definitions in the section labeled "Glossary".

Unless otherwise indicated, I have taken all quotations of Scripture from the *King James Version*.

D.R. Olson
28 December 2020

Abbreviations

Genesis	Gen	Matthew	Matt
Exodus	Ex	Mark	Mark
Leviticus	Lev	Luke	Luke
Numbers	Num	John	John
Deuteronomy	Deut	Acts	Acts
Joshua	Josh	Romans	Rom
Judges	Jdg	1 Corinthians	1Cor
Ruth	Ruth	2 Corinthians	2Cor
1 Samuel	1Sam	Galatians	Gal
2 Samuel	2Sam	Ephesians	Eph
1 Kings	1Ki	Philippians	Php
2 Kings	2Ki	Colossians	Col
1 Chronicles	1Ch	1 Thessalonians	1Th
2 Chronicles	2Ch	2 Thessalonians	2Th
Ezra	Ezra	1 Timothy	1Tim
Nehemiah	Ne	2 Timothy	2Tim
Esther	Es	Titus	Titus
Job	Job	Philemon	Phm
Psalms	Ps	Hebrews	Heb
Proverbs	Pr	James	Jas
Ecclesiastes	Ecc	1 Peter	1Pe
Song of Solomon	Sgs	2 Peter	2Pe
Isaiah	Isa	1 John	1John
Jeremiah	Jer	2 John	2John
Lamentations	Lam	3 John	3John
Ezekiel	Eze	Jude	Jude
Daniel	Dan	Revelation	Rev
Hosea	Hos		
Joel	Joel		
Amos	Amos		
Obadiah	Oba		
Jonah	Jnh		
Micah	Mic		
Nahum	Na		
Habakkuk	Hab		
Zephaniah	Zep		
Haggai	Hag		
Zechariah	Zec		
Malachi	Mal		

Introduction

The letter to the Romans is one of the books of the New Testament.
- **When was it written?**
- **Where was it written?**
- **By whom was it written?**
- **To which Romans was it written?**

The author of the letter cites many passages from the Old Testament.
- **What does this indicate about him?**
- **List all the books of the Old Testament that contain verses that he cites in his letter.**

Romans 1

1 "Paul, a servant of Jesus Christ"
- **How does a person serve Jesus Christ?**

"called to be an apostle"
- **What is an "apostle"?**
  ○ 1Cor 12:28; 15:7b. 2Cor 12:12. 2Tim 1:11. Heb 3:1; Mark 3:14–15; Luke 6:13.
- **How many apostles were there?**
  ○ Mark 3:14; Acts 1:26; Rev 21:14; Rom 16:7; 1Cor 15:5,7,9
- **Who called Paul to be an apostle?**
- **How was Paul called?**
  ○ Acts 9:1–22
- **Had Paul aspired to be an apostle?**
  ○ Acts 8:3
- **Could Paul have rejected the call of apostleship?**
- **Are people called to Christ today as clearly as Paul was called then?**
  ○ Verse 6

"separated unto the gospel of God"
- "Gospel" means "good news". **What is the good news?**
- **From what was Paul separated?**

2–4 "holy scriptures"
- **What does "holy" mean?**
- **How do the holy scriptures differ from other writings that contain truth?**
- **By what criteria do we consider writings to be Scripture?**
- Statements of Jesus indicate that the Old Testament was Scripture (see Mark 12:10; Luke 4:21; John 10:35; 13:18; 17:12). But the New Testament was written after His death. **Is the New Testament holy Scripture?**

- If so, then how do we know that this?
- If not, then why should we believe anything in the New Testament?
- Does other Scripture exist outside the Bible?
- Were the original Scriptures without error?
- What is the best translation of the Bible into English?
- Are all versions of the Scriptures that exist today free of error?
  - If so, then are all people who translate or reproduce the Bible under divine inspiration?
  - If not, then can we really trust any copy of the Scriptures, especially translations not even written in the original language?
- Which error is more serious: rejecting writings that are holy Scripture or accepting as holy Scripture writings that are not?

"according to the flesh"

- Though Christ was born "according to the flesh" and was human, He did not sin. **Was it possible for Christ to have sinned or was it impossible because He was also God? In other words, which statement is true:**
  (a) Christ was able not to sin.
  (b) Christ was not able to sin.
  ○ Heb 4:15. Jas 1:13.

"Which he had promised afore by his prophets", "declared to be the Son of God ... by the resurrection from the dead"

- In verses 2 and 4, Paul describes evidence that demonstrates that Jesus is the Son of God. As stated in verse 2, Jesus was the fulfillment of prophecy given years earlier (such as in Zec 9:9; Mal 3:1; Isa 53) to which He himself alluded (see Luke 24:44; John 5:39, 46). As stated in verse 4, Jesus was declared the Son of God by His resurrection (see Acts 17:31). Other miracles that Christ performed and eyewitnesses saw also support this claim (see John 5:36). **What other arguments could you give that support the fact that Jesus is the Christ and the Saviour of the world?**
- **Was the resurrection necessary?**
  ○ 1Cor 15:12–19; John 14:19b
- **What is the significance of the resurrection beyond demonstrating the veracity of Jesus as the Messiah?**

Romans 1

- 1Pet 1:3; 2Tim 1:10; 1Cor 15:14,17, 20–22; Rom 4:25; 10:9; Matt 17:22–23

"with power"
- **How was power demonstrated in the declaration of verse 4?**

5–6 "by whom we have received grace"
- **To whom does "we" refer in verse 5?**
- **What is "grace"?**
- **In what way had those of verse 5 received grace?**
- Paul writes that they had received grace by Jesus Christ. **Must God's grace to humanity always come through Christ?**
- 1Tim 2:5

"for obedience to the faith among all nations"
- **How is a person obedient to the faith?**
- **Does verse 5 imply some relationship between faith and works?**

"for his name"
- **What does it mean for a person to act for the name of Jesus? Is doing something for *his name* different than doing something for *him*?**
- John 1:12; Acts 22:16; Php 2:9

7 "saints"
- **What is a "saint"?**
- **Who are the saints?**
- 1Cor 1:2

8 "I thank my God through Jesus Christ"
- **Why does Paul write "I thank *my* God" instead of just "I thank God …"?**
- **Why does Paul thank God indirectly through Christ?**
- John 14:6; Matt 11:27; Rom 16:27; 1Tim 2:5

"throughout the whole world"
- **Why would the whole world know about the faith of the people at Rome?**

9–10 "with my spirit"
- **Why does Paul add the phrase "with my spirit" to his statement that he is serving?**

"God is my witness"
- **To what degree is God a witness to our lives?**
  ◦ Heb 4:12

"without ceasing"
- In 1Th 5:17 Paul says, "pray without ceasing". Yet it seems that at times people would need to stop praying at least temporarily in order to eat, drink, or sleep. **What exactly does the phrase "without ceasing" mean in these verses?**

11–12 "that I may impart unto you some spiritual gift"
- **How would Paul impart a spiritual gift; isn't God the One who does this?**
  ◦ 1Cor 14:3
- **What are some spiritual gifts?**
  ◦ Rom 12:6–8; 1Cor 12:7–10, 28–30; Eph 4:11
- **Are spiritual gifts the same as spiritual fruits? If not, then what is the difference between them?**
- **What is the fruit of the Spirit?**
  ◦ Gal 5:22–23

13 "but was let hitherto"
- **What does "let hitherto" mean?**
- Paul states in Rom 15:22 that he was "hindered" from visiting the Romans, though he had wanted to come to Rome (Acts 19:21). **Who or what was preventing him from coming to Rome?**
  ◦ Verse 14; Acts 16:6–7; 19:21; 20:22. 1Th 2:18.
- **Why was Paul hindered from coming there?**
  ◦ Rom 15:20–22

"that I might have some fruit"
- **What is the "fruit" of verse 13? Was Paul hungry?**

14–15 "debtor both to the Greeks, and to the barbarians"
- **Why was Paul in debt to the people of verse 14? What was he obligated to do?**
  ◦ Verse 15; 1Cor 9:16
- **Who were the barbarians?**
- **Who were the Greeks? Were they only people from Greece? Or was "Greeks" a more general term that included people of other races?**

16 "ashamed"
- Paul was not shy to preach the gospel. **For what reasons could he have been reluctant to do so?**
  - Acts 14:19; 17:32
- **What are the advantages and disadvantages of sharing the gospel with others? Do the advantages outweigh the disadvantages?**
- **Are Christians sometimes ashamed of the gospel?**
- **Should Christians always boldly proclaim their faith to others?**

"salvation"
- **What is "salvation"? From what are we saved?**
  - Rom 5:9

"to the Jew first, and also to the Greek"
- **Who is the Greek?**

17–18 "the righteousness of God revealed from faith to faith"
- **What is "righteousness"?**
  - Gen 6:9; Pr 20:7; Ecc 7:20; Isa 64:6; Deut 6:25
- **Should we consider atheists who do good works to be "righteous" people?**
  - 1John 2:29
- **What is "faith"?**
  - Heb 11:1
- **What does "revealed from faith to faith" mean?**
  - Rom 3:21–22

"the wrath of God is revealed from heaven against all ungodliness and unrighteousness of men"
- **Is the wrath of God merely anger?**
- **In what way is the wrath of God revealed in the present?**
- **Is the wrath of God revealed against ungodliness and unrighteousness, but not against men themselves?**
- **Does verse 18 pertain to all men or only unbelievers?**

"who hold the truth in unrighteousness"
- **What does "hold the truth in unrighteousness" mean?**

"is revealed"
- **What does the phrase "is revealed" suggest?**
  - Matt 11:25–27
- **Notice the contrast between that which is revealed in verse 17 and that which is revealed in verse 18.**

- Is God's righteousness revealed to everyone?
- Is God's wrath revealed to everyone?

19–21 "that which may be known of God is manifest in them"
- **What does "manifest" mean?**
- **Is that which may be known of God clear to everyone?**
  ○ Acts 17:31b
- **What happens to people who die without ever hearing about Jesus Christ?**

"For the invisible things of him from the creation of the world are clearly seen"
- **What are the "invisible things" of God in verse 20?**
- **How can they be seen clearly if they are invisible?**

"they are without excuse"
- **When and about what might men want to give excuses?**

"darkened"
- **In what ways is "light" an appropriate word to describe life in Christ?**
  ○ John 1:4–9

22–23 "changed the glory of the uncorruptible God"
- **What is "glory"?**

"into an image made like to corruptible man, and to birds, and fourfooted beasts, and creeping things"
- **How was the glory of God changed into an image of the kind described in verse 23?**
- **Do people change the glory of God into an image of this kind today?**
  ○ Acts 19:24–27; Ex 32:3–4; Gen 3:5, Ps 106:19–22
    - Aside: God told the Israelites not to make "any likeness of any thing that is in heaven above, or that is in the earth beneath, or that is in the water under the earth" (Ex 20:4).
      - **Could the Israelites look at such images as long as they didn't make them?**
      - **Does this commandment extend to us as Christians? If so, then should we not draw paintings, take pictures, or make movies? Should we not look at paintings, pictures, or statues or watch television or movies?**

24–28 "worshipped and served the creature"
- **What is "worship"?**
- **How do some people worship and serve the creature today?**

"change the natural use into that which is against nature"
- **What specifically is this use which is against nature?**
- **What does the Bible say about such practices?**
  - 1Cor 6:9; Lev 18:22; Jude 7
- **Are the Scriptures still relevant today or are the practices described in verses 26 and 27 now legitimate?**

"God also gave them up to uncleanness", "God gave them up unto vile affections", "God gave them over to a reprobate mind"
- **In what way does God give people up to vile affections?**
- **Do verses 24–28 suggest that only with the help of God can people maintain purity of mind?**
- **Did God totally abandon the people of verses 21–32?**
- Many believe that they will go to heaven because they have been "good" according to their own consciences. **Is it reasonable to expect God to leave us alone and let us follow our own law, and yet bring us near to Him upon our physical death?**

29–31 "unrighteousness", "fornication", "wickedness", … "implacable", "unmerciful"
- **Can we categorize the characteristics listed in verses 29–31 in any way?**

"without understanding"
- **Is being "without understanding" (verse 31) also morally wrong?**
  - Verse 18b

32 "knowing the judgment of God"
- Verse 32 indicates that people know that the things described in verses 29–31 are wrong and that those who do them are "worthy of death", yet they "have pleasure in" others that do the same. **Why would someone who sins not only fail to admit his wrongdoing, but also approve when others commit the same sins?**
  - Rom 6:23

Romans 2

1-3 "thou art that judgest", "thou ... doest the same things"
- **May we judge other people as long as we do not do the same things for which we judge them?**
  ◦ Matt 7:1–5

4-10 "the goodness of God leadeth thee to repentance"
- **How does the goodness of God lead us to repentance?**
- **Doesn't wrath lead people to repentance more effectively than goodness?**
- **Was God's patience with and kindness to the Jews effective?**

"day of wrath and revelation of the righteous judgment of God"
- Recall the statement of Rom 1:18 that the "wrath of God is revealed". **Are the wrath and judgment of God reserved for one day or are they revealed frequently?**

"goodness of God"
- **Is God kind and loving or angry and wrathful?**
  ◦ Rom 1:18; John 3:16

"Who will render to every man according to his deeds"
- In Matt 6:1–6, Jesus states that those who give alms to be honored by men have received their reward in full, whereas he who gives alms in secret will be repaid by the Father.
  - **How does the Father reward people?**
  - **Will the Father not reward a person who men have already rewarded for a good thing he has done?**
    ◦ Luke 14:12–14
  - **Will the Father not punish a person who men have already punished for a bad thing he has done?**
    ◦ Matt 16:27

"them who ... seek for glory and honor and immortality"
- **Is it selfish to seek for glory and honor and immortality?**

"Tribulation and anguish, upon every soul of man that doeth evil", "glory, honor, and peace, to every man that worketh good"
- **Could verse 10 apply to "good" non-Christians?**
- **Does verse 9 apply to wayward Christians?**

11–16 "the doers of the law shall be justified"
- **What does "justify" mean?**
  - Jer 31:31–34; Heb 10:17
- **To what "law" is Paul referring?**
- Paul refers to "the" law specifically. **Does this suggest that legal codes other than the one to which he refers are invalid?**
- **If a law from human legislators contradicts the law of God, then which one should we obey?**
- **Is it accurate to say that the source of the law that we choose to obey is also the god that we serve, whether that source is the God of Abraham, Isaac, and Jacob or some government?**
- Many people turn to a government to solve their problems (e.g., for provision when unemployed, for medical care when sick, for security against enemies). **Do these people effectively (if not explicitly) regard the government as their god?**
- God gave the law to Israel through His servant Moses. **Would this law be the best one for us to follow today? Could better law come from corrupt human leaders? Do we need extra laws now because the world is more complicated today than it was thousands of years ago?**
  - Deut 4:2
- **Does verse 13 suggest that people can be saved without Jesus Christ, merely by doing the law?**
  - Rom 3:23; 1John 3:4; Jas 2:10; John 1:29; Matt 5:17

"the Gentiles, which have not the law"
- **Do people who do not have the law need to adhere to any moral standards?**
- **What bearing does the law have on Christians? Must believers in Christ obey the law?**

Romans 2

- Rom 3:31; 8:4; Matt 5:17–20. Rom 6:14; 10:4; John 14:15.

"God shall judge the secrets of men"
- We read in verse 16 that God "shall judge the secrets of men", in verse 6 that God "will render to every man according to his deeds", and elsewhere (such as Rom 3:19; 14:12; Matt 12:36; 2Cor 5:10) that everyone (both Jew and Greek) will be held accountable to God. **How can and how will we as Christians be held accountable for our words and deeds if we are justified by Christ and our sins are not remembered?**
- Rom 4:7–8; Heb 8:12; John 3:18.

"my gospel"
- **Why does Paul write "*my* gospel" instead of "*the* gospel"?**
- Gal 1:11–12; Rom 16:25; 2Tim 2:8.

17–20 "restest in the law"
- **How do "Jews" rest in the law?**
- **Is the law useless if it cannot produce salvation?**
- Rom 8:3–4

21–24 "For the name of God is blasphemed among the Gentiles through you"
- **What does "blaspheme" mean?**
- **How would the hypocritical actions of the Jews cause Gentiles to blaspheme?**
- Eze 36:16–23; 2Cor 6:3

25–26 "thy circumcision is made uncircumcision"
- **What is the meaning of circumcision becoming uncircumcision?**
- Jer 4:4; 9:25–26; verse 29; Deut 10:16

"shall not his uncircumcision be counted for circumcision"
- **What is the meaning of uncircumcision being counted for circumcision?**
- **Who would count uncircumcision for circumcision?**

27–29 "if it fulfil the law, judge thee, who ... dost transgress the law?"
- Verse 27 states that those who fulfill the law will judge those who transgress of the law. **Why isn't such judg-**

ment inconsistent with the warnings against passing judgment that Paul expresses in verses 1–3?
- ◦ Verse 16; John 5:22, 27; Matt 19:28; 1Cor 6:2–3
- **When will judgment by those who fulfill the law take place?**

"he is not a Jew, which is one outwardly", "he is a Jew, which is one inwardly"

- In verse 17, Paul writes "thou art called a Jew", not "thou art a Jew". By this phrase and his statements in verses 28 and 29, he seems to indicate that "Jewishness" is not a matter of ethnic background (also Rev 2:9; 3:9). **Does being a "Jew" by birth have any significance?**
- ◦ Rom 3:1–2
- According to Paul, he who is truly a Jew "keeps the righteousness of the law" (verse 26), fulfills the law (verse 27), will judge the transgressors of the law (verse 27), and has a "circumcision ... of the heart, in the spirit" (verse 29). **What people fulfill these criteria?**
- ◦ Jas 2:8, 10; Rom 8:4, 9; Php 3:2–3; Col 2:11; 1Cor 6:2–3
- **Should the way in which we define who is a "Jew" affect how we regard God's promises in the Old Testament?**
- ◦ Eph 2:11–13; Gal 3:14
- Aside: Paul mentions elsewhere "promises made unto the fathers" (Rom 15:8). **What promises did God make to the Jews?**
- ◦ Ex 3:8; Deut 15:4–6; Acts 13:23

Romans 3

1–2 "the Jew", "circumcision"
- In verse 1, is Paul referring to those who are Jews outwardly (the "circumcised of flesh") or to those who are Jews inwardly (the "circumcised of heart")?

"unto them were committed the oracles of God"
- What are "oracles"?
- What were the "oracles of God" that were committed unto the Jews?
- What did this commitment require of the Jews?
- Did they violate this commitment?
- Why was being committed with the oracles of God an advantage?

"chiefly"
- Are there any other advantages for the Jew?
  - If not, then why does Paul write "chiefly"?
  - If so, then what are they?

3 "faith of God"
- Does "faith of God" in verse 3 mean:
  (a) Faith in God?
  (b) Faith that God has in something?
  (c) Faithfulness of God?
  (d) Something else?
- In what ways is God faithful?
  ○ Jdg 2:1; Deut 7:9. Josh 21:45; 23:14; Ne 9:8; 1Ki 8:56. 1John 1:9; 1Cor 10:13.
- Does God owe us anything?

4 "when thou art judged"
- How could God be judged?

5 "Is God unrighteous who taketh vengeance?"
- **Can a loving God cast people into the lake of fire?**
  - Verses 6–8, 26; John 5:30; Heb 2:2–3; Ex 3:5–6; Rev 20:15

9 "are we better than they?"
- **To whom do "we" and "they" refer in verse 9?**

"are all under sin"
- **What is "sin"?**
  - Jas 4:17

10–18 "Their throat is an open sepulchre"
- **In what way was their throat an open sepulchre?**
  - Matt 15:18; 23:27–28

"Their feet are swift to shed blood"
- **How do feet shed blood?**
  - Pr 1:16

19 "that every mouth may be stopped"
- **What should every mouth be stopped from saying?**
  - Verse 27

20 "by the deeds of the law there shall no flesh be justified in his sight: for by the law is the knowledge of sin"
- **Is justification impossible without Christ merely because we have a knowledge of what sin is?**
- **Without the law would we not be sinful creatures?**
  - Rom 4:15; 5:13; 7:7; John 9:41; Luke 12:48; 1John 3:4
- In Gen 2:9, 16–17; 3:6–7, 22–23, we read that once Adam and Eve ate from the tree, they knew of their nakedness and their sin. **Were Adam and Eve expelled from the Garden of Eden because they disobeyed God or because they now had this knowledge?**
  - **Aside: Was it mostly the woman's fault?**
  - **Aside: To whom does "us" refer in Gen 3:22?**

21 "the righteousness of God ... is manifested, being witnessed by the law and the prophets"
- **How was the righteousness of God manifested?**
- **How did the law and the prophets witness the righteousness of God?**
  - Matt 11:13; John 1:45; 5:46–47; Luke 16:27–31

- Aside: In Matt 11:13, Jesus states that "all the prophets and the law prophesied until John". **Did they discontinue prophesying after this point?**
    - If so, then:
        - **Were the prophets and the law invalidated after John?**
        - **Is the gift of prophecy no longer dispensed by the Holy Spirit and has it not been dispensed since the days of John?**
    - **If not, then why did Jesus use the word "prophesied" in the past tense?**
  - Acts 21:12; 1Cor 14:39; Luke 24:44,27

22 "there is no difference"
- **Between what is there no difference?**
  - Verse 9

23 "all have sinned"
- **Do the phrases "all have sinned" (verse 23) and "are all under sin" (verse 9) have the same meaning?**

24 "redemption"
- **What is "redemption"?**
  - Mark 10:45; Eph 4:30

25 "Whom God hath set forth to be a propitiation through faith in his blood"
- **What is a "propitiation"?**

"in his blood", "for the remission of sins"
- We read in Heb 9:22 that "without shedding of blood is no remission". **Why are sacrifice and the shedding of blood necessary for the remission of sins?**
  - Gen 2:17

"remission of sins that are past"
- **Are Christ's death and resurrection relevant to those who died before He came?**
  - Heb 10:1–4, 11–12; John 5:25, 28–29; 1Pe 4:6

26 "that he might be just"
- **In what way does the act described in verse 25 show God to be just?**

- Lev 26:14–21, 40–45; Rom 3:5–6; 2:5–6; Heb 2:2; 1John 1:9
- **Was it just for God to send His innocent Son to die and bear the punishment for our sins?**
- Matt 26:39. Matt 26:51–54; John 1:1; 10:30.

27–30 "Where is boasting then?"
- **Why does man have no reason to boast?**
- Eph 2:8–9

"law of faith"
- **What is a "law of faith"?**

31 "we establish the law"
- **How does verse 31 reconcile with Rom 10:4?**

Romans 4

1 "that Abraham our father, as pertaining to the flesh, hath found"
- **Does verse 1 indicate that Abraham is our father pertaining to the flesh or that Abraham has found something that pertains to the flesh?**
- **What did Abraham find?**
  ◦ Verse 11

4–5 "to him that worketh not, but believeth"
- **Do believers not perform good works?**

"on him that justifieth the ungodly"
- In verse 5, we read that Christ justifies the ungodly who believe in Him. But in Ex 23:7, the Lord said to Moses, "I will not justify the wicked". **Has God changed?**

"his faith is counted for righteousness"
- In contrast with verse 4, verse 5 indicates that righteousness is reckoned as a gift that comes through belief, not as a wage (something earned) that comes through works. **Do verses 4–5 suggest that there are two types of people who are reckoned as righteous: those who believe (whose righteousness is reckoned as a gift) and those who do good works (whose righteousness is earned as a wage)?**
  ◦ Eph 2:8–9; Rom 6:23

6–8 "blessedness", "Blessed"
- **What does it mean to be "blessed"?**

9–12 "faith was reckoned to Abraham for righteousness"
- **In what ways did Abraham demonstrate faith?**
  ◦ Gen 15:1–6; 12:1–5; 22:1–18

- Aside: What events does Gen 22:1–18 foreshadow?
- Aside: Does "seed" in Gen 22:16–18 refer to Isaac?
  - Gal 3:16

"the sign of circumcision, a seal of the righteousness of the faith"

- What is a "seal"?
- In what sense was circumcision a seal?
- Do believers receive any kind of seal of righteousness through faith?
- 2Cor 1:22; Eph 1:13; 4:30; Luke 24:49
- Is a seal of righteousness permanent?
- John 10:27–30. 1Sam 16:14.
- What is the value of a seal of righteousness?
- If a person believes and confesses that Jesus Christ is Lord at some point in time, then is he guaranteed eternal life regardless of his actions in the future? What if he later openly rejects Christ?
- Circumcision was an outward sign of Abraham's righteousness through faith. **Do believers show an outward sign of righteousness through faith in Christ?**
  - Gal 5:22–23; John 15:8

"the father of all them that believe"

- In what way is Abraham the father of believers? Isn't God the Father of believers, having adopted them as His children (Rom 8:14–15)?

"them ... who walk in the steps of that faith of our father Abraham"

- Paul seems to suggest in this passage that there was a place for faith between Abraham's lifetime and Christ's appearance on earth. **In what should that faith have been, since Christ had not yet come?**
- Would such faith have any redeeming value?
  - If so, then why did Christ need to come?
  - If not, then what would be the value of such faith?

13–15 "heir of the world"

- In Matt 5:5, Jesus said "Blessed are the meek: for they shall inherit the earth". In verse 13, Paul seems to suggest that people of faith are the heirs of the world. **Does this mean that the meek are the people of faith? Are meekness and faith related?**

Romans 4

- Aside: Are the Beatitudes (Matt 5:3–10) relevant to Christians only or to all people with the attitudes described?

"faith is made void, and the promise made of none effect"
- Why would the promise and faith become null and void if those who are of the law are heirs?

"the law worketh wrath: for where no law is, there is no transgression"
- Is the law the only means by which we can recognize transgression and sin? Can't we trust our consciences to discern between right and wrong?
  ○ Rom 7:7
- Were violations of commandments that occurred before God gave the law to Moses, such as the murder of Abel by Cain (Gen 4:8), still transgressions?
  - If so, then would the violators have known that their actions were wrong?
    - If so, then how would they know?
    - If not, then why should they receive any punishment?
  - If not, then why were violators (e.g., Cain, the Sodomites, the people alive when Noah built the ark) punished?
- Did God make known his law before Moses, just not in written form?

16–17 "that it might be by grace"
- Why is grace so critical?

"the promise might be sure to all the seed; not to that only which is of the law, but to that also which is of the faith of Abraham"
- Who are those "of the law"?
- Who are those "of the faith of Abraham"?
  ○ Verse 12
- Does verse 16 indicate that the promise is sure to all those of the law (even the faithless)?

"a father of many nations"
- Of which nations is Abraham a father?

18–22 "against hope believed in hope", "his own body now dead"
- Abraham's condition was utterly hopeless without the

intervention of God. **Does this describe our condition as sinners as well or do we have better prospects?**
- ○ Eph 2:1, 5, 12

"being not weak in faith"
- Abraham recognized his own sorry condition, yet he "staggered not ... through unbelief; but was strong in faith". **Can Abraham serve as an example to us or is his situation too different from ours?**

23–25 "it was not written for his sake alone ... but for us also"
- **In verse 23, what is "it" that was written for us?**
- **In what way was it written for us?**
- **Given that the book of Genesis was not written until after the death of Abraham, in what way was it written for his sake at all?**
- **As Christians, how much of the Old Testament was written "for us also"? Is the Old Testament useful to us or is it obsolete?**
- ○ 2Tim 3:15–16
- **Should preachers give sermons on passages in the Old Testament or should they focus on the New Testament to the exclusion of the Old?**

"if we believe on him"
- **What does it mean to believe "on" someone?**
- We read in Gen 15:6 that Abram "believed in the Lord". **Do the phrases "believe on (the Lord)" (verse 24), "believe in the Lord" (Gen 15:6), and "believe (the Lord)" (verse 3) differ in meaning?**

"delivered for our offenses"
- **How, where, to whom, and by whom was Jesus delivered for our offenses?**
- ○ Rom 8:32

Romans 5

1 "justified by faith"
   - **In what must we place our faith to be justified?**
   - ○ Rom 4:24

   "we have peace with God"
   - **If we as believers have peace with God only after we are justified, then what was our relationship to Him before we were justified?**
   - ○ Verse 10; Rom 8:7; Matt 12:30

2 "access by faith into this grace"
   - **What does access into God's grace entail?**
   - Paul also uses the word "access" in Eph 2:18 and 3:12 to describe our relationship with the Father. **Did anyone have access to the Father in the age before Christ came?**
   - ○ Heb 9:1–7
   - **How did the means of access before Christ foreshadow the means of access now?**
   - ○ Heb 9:11–12, 23–25
   - **Do Matt 27:50–51 and Heb 10:19–23 suggest that we now have direct, unmediated access to the Father?**
     - **If so, then do we need Christ any longer beyond the moment of our conversion?**
     - **If not, then what does the tearing of the veil of the temple described in Matt 27:51 signify?**
   - ○ Heb 9:24; 1Tim 2:5

3–4 "tribulation worketh patience; and ... hope"
   - **Can non-Christians progress through stages of tribulation, patience, experience, and hope?**
   - Paul also writes in Rom 15:4 that "we through patience

and comfort of the Scriptures might have hope". **With what do Christians need patience and in what should Christians hope?**
- Acts 14:21–22; Jas 1:1–4. Verse 2.
- **How does tribulation lead to patience?**
- **How does patience lead to experience?**
- **How does experience lead to hope?**

"we glory in tribulations"
- **What does it mean to "glory" in tribulations?**
- **By "tribulations", does Paul mean trials of any kind or trials of some specific kind (such as persecution for confessing faith in Christ)?**
- **How can we glory in tribulations? Don't tribulations depress us?**

5 "And hope maketh not ashamed; because the love of God is shed abroad in our hearts by the Holy Ghost"
- **Of what does hope make not ashamed?**
- **How is the love of God "shed abroad" in our hearts through the Holy Spirit?**
- Joel 2:28; Titus 3:5–6; 1John 2:27; Isa 32:15–17; Lev 8:12
- **Why does the shedding abroad of the love of God mean that "hope maketh not ashamed"?**
- Rom 2:29; 4:11; Eph 1:13

6–8 "when we were yet without strength"
- **What were we without strength to do?**

"while we were yet sinners"
- **Why does Paul write "we were *yet* without strength" and "we were *yet* sinners" instead of "we were without strength" and "we were sinners"? In other words, how does the inclusion of the word "yet" change the meaning of the phrases?**

"in due time Christ died for the ungodly", "Christ died for us"
- Christ died roughly two thousand years ago. **Why did He come and die at that particular time? Why not earlier or later? Was there something special about that era that made it the proper time?**
- Gal 4:4; Mark 1:15
- **How could the death of a single man cover the sins of**

millions of people?
- ○ 2Cor 5:14
- One might be willing to die for a good man, but how could one be willing to die for a mass murderer, a torturer, a thief, or an enemy?
- How does the death of Christ demonstrate the love of God?
- ○ Rom 8:32; John 3:16

9–11 "Much more then"
- Paul states in verses 9–10 that much more shall we be saved beyond justification and reconciliation. **What is the nature of such greater salvation? After we are justified and reconciled, in what manner does God's relationship with us develop further through the resurrected and living Christ?**
- Is a strengthening of a Christian's relationship to God through Christ after conversion:
  (a) Required (to gain eternal life)?
  (b) Inevitable?
  (c) Commonplace?
  (d) Rare?

"justified by his blood"
- Verses 9–10 indicate that we are justified by the blood of Christ through His death. Rom 4:25 contains the phrase "raised again for our justification". **Are Christians justified through the death of Christ or through the resurrection of Christ? Are Christians cleansed from sin by the death of Jesus or by the living Jesus?**
- ○ Heb 9:22; 1John 1:9

"we shall be saved"
- The tense of "shall be saved" is future. **Have we been saved already or will we be saved at a later time?**
- ○ Mark 16:16; John 10:9; Heb 1:14. Eph 2:5; 2Tim 1:8–9; Titus 3:5; Luke 19:9. 1Cor 15:2; 2Cor 2:15; Heb 7:25.

"reconciled", "saved"
- **Are reconciliation/justification and salvation different positions in relation to God? Are we first reconciled, then saved? Or are we reconciled, justified, and saved all at the same time?**
- If we as Christians were justified and reconciled to

God through Christ's death, then why would we need to be saved from God's wrath? In other words, against what in us could God's wrath be revealed if our sins have been forgiven and remembered no more?
- Jer 31:34

"when we were enemies"
- **Are all people without Christ at enmity with God?**
- Rom 1:18–19; Col 1:19–22; Jas 4:4
- **Was this enmity of verse 10 bilateral or unilateral? That is, did God hate us while we hated Him or did God love us even while we hated Him?**
- Verse 8; John 3:16; 1John 4:10

12–14 "as by one man sin entered into the world"
- **Who is the man of verse 12?**
- Verse 14

"and death by sin"
- Both verse 12 and Gen 2:16–17 imply that before the sin of one man there was no death. **To what kind of death do these verses refer? A loss of life in our perishable bodies? A loss of eternal life?**
- **Why is death a necessary consequence of sin? Could not God exact a less severe penalty?**
- Gen 2:17
- **Will those in Christ not experience death?**
- 2Cor 5:14; Col 3:3; 2Tim 2:11; Rom 6:6

"sin is not imputed when there is no law"
- **What does "impute" mean?**

"sinned after the similitude of Adam's transgression"
- **What sins are like the transgression of Adam?**

"Nevertheless death reigned from Adam until Moses"
- **If God gave the law through Moses and "sin is not imputed when there is no law", then why did death reign nevertheless between the time of Adam and the time of Moses?**

"death passed upon all men, for that all have sinned"
- Paul states in 1Cor 15:22 that "in Adam all die" and indicates in verse 12 that in Adam all die because in Adam all sinned. **In what way did we sin in Adam?**
- **Is it fair that death should come to us because of Adam's sin? Shouldn't we be punished only for our**

own sins?
- Christ was born of a human woman (Mary). **Why was He not charged with sinning in Adam?**
- Does the idea that all sinned in Adam suggest that a man descended from Adam who had not himself committed sin would still be guilty?
    - If not, then is salvation by works theoretically possible?
    - If so, then does this add significance to the virgin birth of Christ?
- If in Adam all sinned and death has passed to all men, then how is sin ever "not imputed" (verse 13)?

"the figure of him that was to come"
- What is a "figure"?
- How is Adam a figure of Jesus Christ?
  - 1Cor 15:21–22. Gen 1:27; 4:1; Rom 8:29 ("first born"); John 14:6. Gen 1:26–28; John 16:2.
- What other figures appear in the Old Testament?

15–19 "But not as the offense, so also is the free gift"
- What contrasts between the free gift and the offense is Paul trying to emphasize?

"the judgment was by one to condemnation"
- Does "one" in verse 16 refer to one man or one offense?
  - Gen 3:6; verses 17, 19

"by the righteousness of one the free gift came upon all men unto justification of life"
- Does "one" in verse 18 refer to one man or one act?
- What was the free gift?
- How did the righteousness of one bring the free gift?
  - Matt 26:38–39; 27:50; Php 2:8
- Did the free gift come upon all men or only the elect?

"shall many be made righteous"
- In verse 18 we read that the free gift "came" (past tense) upon all men unto justification, but in verse 19 we read that many "shall" (future tense) be made righteous. **Are believers righteous now by virtue of being justified or will believers be made righteous only later?**

20 "the law entered, that the offense might abound"

- **Was the purpose of the law to cause an increase in sin?**
  - 1Cor 15:56

21 "so might grace reign through righteousness unto eternal life by Jesus Christ our Lord"
- **What is "eternal life"?**
  - John 17:3

Romans 6

1–2 "Shall we continue in sin ... ?"
- Paul asks similar questions in verses 1 and 15. **If we as Christians are justified and declared righteous by God, then:**
  - **Does it matter ultimately if we sin?**
  - **Do we have anything to lose by sinning?**
  - **Do we need to ask for forgiveness for our sins?**
- ○ Matt 5:12; 16:27; 1Cor 3:11–15; 2Tim 2:11–13

3 "baptized into Jesus Christ"
- **What does "baptize" mean?**
- The phrase "baptized into" appears as well in verse 3; 1Cor 12:13; Gal 3:27. **What does it mean to be "baptized into" something?**
- The phrase "baptized with" appears in Matt 3:11; Mark 10:38; Acts 11:16. **What does it mean to be "baptized with" something?**
- **How are we baptized into Christ Jesus?**
- ○ Acts 1:5; 11:16; 1Cor 12:12–13; John 1:33
- Does Jesus imply in Mark 16:16 that a physical baptism with water is required for salvation?
  - **If so, then is baptism essentially a work by which we save ourselves?**
  - If not, then:
    - Why does Jesus say "and has been baptized"?
    - Is baptism important?
      - **If so, then what is the significance of baptism with water?**
      - **If not, then why do some churches perform baptisms and require baptism for membership?**

- Matt 10:32; Luke 12:50; Rom 10:9; 1Pe 3:21
- **What was the significance of baptism with water before the death and resurrection of Christ (especially in the work of John the Baptist)?**
- Mark 1:8; Luke 3:3; Acts 19:4
- **Was baptism a common practice before John or was he the first person to baptize people?**
- According to 1Cor 12:27, believers are members of the body of Christ. **After conversion, do believers remain in Christ always?**
    - **If so, then why did Jesus need to tell his disciples to "abide in me" (John 15:4)?**
    - **If not, then:**
        - **How could believers in Christ become separated from him?**
        - **What are the consequences of not remaining in Christ?**
- 1John 3:6; 4:13; 2:24. Heb 6:4–6; 1Tim 1:19; 6:10; John 15.

4–9 "we are buried with him"
- **In what way are people buried with Christ?**
- Verse 6
- **Will Christians be buried with Christ until the resurrection? Do Christians have eternal life at the present time?**

"walk in newness of life"
- **What does it mean to "walk in newness of life"?**
- Eph 4:20–24; Col 3:9–11; Eze 36:26–27; 2Cor 4:16
- **Read 2Cor 4:16. How is our inward man "renewed day by day"?**
- 1Pe 1:2; Titus 3:5
- **Should people see evidence that Christians walk in "newness of life"?**
- Gal 5:22–25

"our old man", "body of sin"
- **What exactly is our "old man"?**

"he that is dead is freed from sin"
- **Is disregard of moral inhibitions also a kind of "freedom from sin"?**

"death hath no more dominion over him"

- Christians still die physically. **Does death continue to have dominion over us as Christians?**
- **If we are justified through Christ, then why do our physical bodies continue to decay?**

10–14 "died unto sin", "sin shall not have dominion over you"
- **What does it mean to "die unto" something?**
- Verse 6 says that "we should not serve sin", verse 7 mentions being "freed from sin", and verse 11 states that we should reckon ourselves "dead indeed unto sin". **What future experience with sin will we have if we have died with Christ to sin? Will we never sin again? Will we continue to sin? Can we become enslaved again to sin?**
    - If we no longer commit sin, then how does the charge in 1John 1:10 relate to us?
    - If we do still commit sin, then:
        - Why do we still commit sin, given that we have died to sin with Christ?
        - How can any of us not be enslaved to sin, given John 8:34?
        - Does God justify us once for all time upon our acceptance of Christ or do we require justification repeatedly (or even continually) after our conversion?
  ○ 1John 1:7, 9; Heb 9:14

"Neither yield ye your members as instruments of unrighteousness unto sin"
- **Why doesn't Paul more simply write "do not sin" in the first part of verse 13?**

15–18 "servants ... of sin ... or of obedience"
- **What is a "servant of obedience"? By definition, isn't a servant a person who obeys?**
- **Is everyone either a "servant of sin" or a "servant of obedience"?**
- **Which kind of servant is the non-Christian who tries to adhere to "Christian" moral standards but stumbles as Christians do?**
  ○ Verse 7

"obedience unto righteousness"

- Does the phrase "obedience unto righteousness" in verse 16 imply that people can be saved by works?
- Does the phrase imply that good works are necessary for salvation?
  ◦ John 3:36; Rom 3:28; Eph 2:8–9; Gal 2:16

"ye have obeyed from the heart"
- What is the difference between obedience "from the heart" and simply obedience?
  ◦ Heb 10:16–17; Jer 31:33–34; Eze 36:24–31

"that form of doctrine"
- What is the "form of doctrine" of verse 17?

19–23 "I speak after the manner of men"
- Why did Paul say that he speaks "after the manner of men"? After what other manner would he speak?

"ye have your fruit unto holiness"
- What is the "fruit" of verse 22?
- What distinguishes a person who is holy from a person who is not holy?
  ◦ Lev 8:30; 20:7–8; 21:8; 2Tim 2:20–21; Heb 9:13–14; Eph 5:25–27
- How are we made holy? Do we make ourselves holy through obedience and good works?
  ◦ Rom 15:16; 2Th 2:13; 1Cor 1:2; Heb 2:11; 13:12; 1Th 5:23; Titus 3:5; 1Pet 1:2; Heb 9:13–14
- Do we become holy at an instant or over a period of time? Are we holy now or will we be made holy later?
  ◦ 1Cor 1:2; 6:11; Heb 2:11; 10:10, 14, 29. Rom 6:19, 22; 1Th 5:23; 2Cor 7:1.
  - Aside #1: In 1Cor 7:14, we read that an unbeliever is sanctified through his or her spouse. **What does "sanctify" mean? Does 1Cor 7:14 indicate that not everyone needs to believe in Christ personally to be saved?**
  - Aside #2: In John 17:19, we read that Christ sanctified Himself for the sakes of the men to whom God had given Him out of the world. **What does this mean?**

Romans 7

1–3 "For the woman which hath a husband is bound ... though she be married to another man"
- **How do the people in verses 2–3 relate to the people of verse 4?**
  - **To what/whom does the (first) husband relate?**
  - **To what/whom does the other man relate?**
  - **To what/whom does the woman relate?**
  - **To what/whom does the law relate?**
  ○ Rom 6:4–6; 10–11. Rom 7:25–8:2.

4–6 "that ye should be married to another"
- **To what/whom were we married before Christ?**
- **In what way is the relationship between Christ and the church similar to the relationship between a husband and wife?**
  ○ Eph 5:23; 2Cor 11:2–3; 1Cor 7:39, 14

"For when we were in the flesh, the motions of sins ... did work in our members"
- Paul uses the past tense in verse 5. **But are we not in the flesh now? Do not the motions of sins still work in our members?**
  ○ Rom 8:9

7–8 "Is the law sin?"
- **If sin and wrath result from the law (Rom 4:15; 5:20), then why would we want the law?**

"Thou shalt not covet"
- **Did Paul use the particular commandment "thou shalt not covet" in his illustration for a reason? Is this commandment of a different kind than the others?**
  ○ Ex 20:1–17

"sin, taking occasion", "wrought", "sin revived" (verse 9)
- **For what purpose does Paul personify sin?**
- **How did sin "take occasion" through the commandment?**
  ○ Verse 5; 1Cor 15:56b
- **If the commandment had not been given, then would no one covet?**

"without the law sin was dead"
- In chapter 6, Paul writes that we should reckon ourselves dead to sin. **What is the difference between sin being dead (verse 8) and we being dead to sin (Rom 6:11)?**

9–13 "I was alive without the law once"
- **In verse 9, does "alive" mean having physical life or having spiritual life?**
- **Isn't the idea of being alive without the law inconsistent with Rom 5:12–14, in which Paul says that "death passed upon all men"?**
- **How could the commandment be "ordained to life" (verse 10) when Paul was already "alive" without it (verse 9)?**
  ○ Rom 2:12; 4:15

"when the commandment came"
- **When did the commandment come? Is Paul suggesting in verse 9 that it came in his own lifetime?**

"the commandment, which was ordained to life"
- **Which commandment was ordained to life? By "commandment" does Paul mean the law in general?**
  ○ Verses 7–8
- **How was the commandment ordained to life?**

"I died", "I found to be unto death", "slew me"
- **In what way could a living person have already died, sin having killed him?**
  ○ Gen 2:16–17

"Was then that which is good made death unto me?", "sin, working death in me"
- In verse 11 we read that "sin, taking occasion by the commandment ... slew me", but in verse 13 Paul implies that the commandment did *not* make "death unto me". **Do these verses contradict each other?**

"For sin ... deceived me"
- **How does sin deceive through commandments?**
  ○ Verse 13; Gen 3:13

"that sin by the commandment might become exceeding sinful"
- **What does it mean for sin to become "exceeding sinful"? How sinful can sin be?**
- **Why does Paul continue to emphasize "the commandment" instead of the law in general?**
  ○ Jas 2:10–11

14–23 "the law is spiritual: but I am carnal"
- **What does verse 14 imply?**
  ○ John 3:6; Gal 5:16–17
- **In what way is the law spiritual?**

"no more I that do it, but sin that dwelleth in me"
- **In verse 17, is Paul trying to avoid taking responsibility for his actions?**
- **Does the claim that sin "dwelleth in me" provide us with a legitimate excuse to sin?**
  ○ Rom 8:9; Eph 4:20–24; Col 3:9–10; 1John 3:6, 9; 5:18
    - Aside: Read 1John 3:6, 9; 5:18. **How do these verses reconcile with 1John 1:8–10?**

"in me (that is, in my flesh,) dwelleth no good thing"
- **How does Paul clarify his statement by adding "in my flesh"?**
  ○ Rom 8:9; Matt 26:41

"sin that dwelleth in me", "evil is present with me"
- In Rom 8:9 we read that the Spirit of God dwells in us as Christians. **Can sin and evil dwell in us even while we are indwelt by the Holy Spirit?**
- **Can Christians become possessed by demons?**

"inward man"
- **What exactly is the "inward man"?**
- **What would be the "outward man"?**
  ○ Verses 23–25; 2Cor 4:16

24–25 "deliver me from the body of this death"
- **What is *this* death? Is Paul referring to some particular kind of death?**
- A Christian is still in his body and will still physically

die. **How can Christians be delivered from their bodies?**
- 1Cor 15:40–55
- **Is Paul suggesting in verses 24-25 that Christ delivers Christians from their bodies?**
  - Aside: In 1Cor 15:42, we read of the resurrection of the dead where the body is "sown a perishable body" and "raised an imperishable body". **In light of this statement, should we not cremate corpses?**

"I thank God through Jesus Christ our Lord!"
- **How does Paul's statement of thanks in verse 25 relate to verses 14–24?**

"I myself serve ... with the flesh the law of sin"
- **Why does Paul write "I myself" here instead of simply "I", as written in each of verses 14–24?**
- **Is Paul saying in verse 25 that Christians necessarily serve both the law of God and the law of sin?**
- Rom 6:6–7, 10–12; 8:9, 12–13; Matt 6:24

7–24 "I", "me"
- **Is Paul discussing himself in verses 7–24?**
  - **If so, then:**
    - **How does Paul's admission that in him was all manner of concupiscence (verse 8) relate to Php 3:6, in which he says he was blameless?**
    - **Given his Jewish background (Acts 22:3; Php 3:5), when was he alive without the law (verse 9)? When did the commandment come to him (verse 9)?**
    - **How can he say that he himself practices sin and evil and cannot help himself (verses 15, 19), where elsewhere he says not to let sin reign and not to obey its lusts (Rom 6:1–2, 6–7, 12–13; Gal 5:16)?**
    - **Why does he speak now of being captive to the law of sin (verse 23), when he speaks elsewhere about having been freed from sin and the law of sin (Rom 6:18; 8:2)?**
  - **If not, then what does he mean when he uses the pronoun "I"?**

Romans 8

1 "There is therefore now no condemnation to them which are in Christ Jesus"
   - **Why is there now no condemnation for them who are in Christ Jesus.**
     - Verse 2; Rom 5:16–18; John 5:24

2 "the law of the Spirit of life in Christ Jesus hath made me free from the law of sin and death"
   - **What is the law of the Spirit of life?**
   - **What is the law of sin and death?**
   - **Are either of these laws the same as the law that is holy of Rom 7:12?**
   - **How did the one law make Paul free from the other?**
     - Rom 6:7, 10–11; 7:1–6; Gal 5:1

3 "what the law could not do"
   - **What could the law not do?**
     - Rom 7:10
   "in the likeness of sinful flesh"
   - **Why is the phrase "in the likeness" necessary here?**
     - Rom 5:12; 2Cor 5:21; 1Pe 2:22

4–5 "that the requirement of the law might be fulfilled in us, who walk not after the flesh"
   - **How does Paul's assertion in verse 4 that he does not walk after the flesh relate to his statement in Rom 7:19 that he does evil?**
   - **What was the requirement of the law?**
     - Jas 2:8–10
   - **Why was this required of us?**
     - Rom 3:26

"walk ... after the flesh", "are after the flesh"
- **Is there any difference between *walking* after the flesh (verse 4) and *being* after the flesh (verse 5)?**
  ○ Verse 9; Rom 6:4; John 8:12; Gal 5:16–25; 2John 6

6–8 "to be carnally minded is death", "to be spiritually minded is life and peace"
- **Why does Paul say that to be carnally minded *is* death instead of *leads to* death (or something similar)?**
  ○ John 3:36; 6:47; 17:3

"they that are in the flesh cannot please God"
- **Does verse 8 suggest that gifts of charity or forms of aid from non-believers do not please God?**
- **Do religions other than Christianity have any value?**
  ○ Heb 11:6; Jas 2:19

9–10 "ye are not in the flesh"
- **How can we be not in the flesh while we still have our earthly bodies?**
  ○ John 3:6

"the Spirit of God dwell in you"
- We find descriptions of the gift of the Holy Spirit in Rom 5:5 and Acts 2:1–4. **Can this Spirit leave us?**
  ○ Verse 16; Eph 1:13–14
- **Do the phrases "Spirit of God dwell in you", "have ... the Spirit of Christ", and "Christ be in you" all have the same meaning?**
  ○ Eph 3:17; Col 1:27–28; 2:9–12
- Paul mentions in verses 9–10 that the "Spirit of God" and "Christ" are in us. In other verses (e.g., Rom 8:1; 1Th 4:16; 1Cor 1:30) he mentions that we are in Christ. **What is the difference between Christ being in us and we being in Christ?**

"the body is dead because of sin"
- **Is the body dead right now?**
  ○ Rom 4:19

"but the Spirit is life because of righteousness"
- **How is the Spirit life because of righteousness?**
  ○ Rom 1:17; Matt 5:20; 25:34–46

11 "he that raised up Christ from the dead shall also quicken

your mortal bodies"
- **When will he that raised up Christ quicken our mortal bodies? Does this verse refer to a resurrection?**
  ◦ Rom 6:5; 1Cor 6:14; 15:42–44

12 "we are debtors"
- **To whom or what are believers in debt?**
- **Must believers repay this debt?**

13 "if ye live after the flesh, ye shall die"
- **To what kind of death does verse 13 refer?**
  - **If it refers to loss of life in our perishable bodies, then does the verse imply that those who walk after the Spirit will not die in this way?**
  - **If it refers to a loss of eternal life, then is it even possible for Christians to live after the flesh, since those in Christ will inherit eternal life?**
    - **If so, then do Christians have no guarantee of eternal life?**
    - **If not, then why does Paul even make this statement?**

  ◦ 1Pe 3:18; Eze 33:13–15; Rom 6:13, 16

"mortify the deeds of the body"
- **How do we "mortify" the deeds of the body"?**

14–18 "as many as are led by the Spirit of God, they are the sons of God"
- **Are all Christians led by the Spirit of God?**
- **Are people who "quench" (1Th 5:19) or "grieve" (Eph 4:30) the Spirit sons of God?**

  ◦ Gal 5:16–18; 4:4–7

"sons of God", "children of God"
- **What is the difference between "sons of God" (verse 14) and "children of God" (verse 16)?**

  ◦ John 3:3; 1Cor 3:1–3; Gal 3:26–4:7

"again to fear"
- **What do those with the spirit of bondage fear?**

"we cry, Abba, Father"
- **Why is the word "Abba" not translated into English (as "Father") in verse 15?**

  ◦ Mark 14:36

"The Spirit itself beareth witness with our spirit"
- **How does the Spirit bear witness with our spirit?**

"ye", "we"
- In verse 15, Paul uses "ye" in stating that his readers "have not received the spirit of bondage" but "have received the Spirit of adoption", but he uses "we" in describing who cries out. **What does the change in pronouns signify?**
  ○ Verse 16

"heirs of God, and joint-heirs with Christ"
- **As heirs, what do we inherit?**
  ○ Matt 19:29

"if so be that we suffer with him, that we may be also glorified together"
- **How do we suffer with Christ?**
- **What does "glorify" mean?**
  ○ Php 1:6; 2Th 2:13–14; Heb 2:10–11; 1Pe 5:1, 4, 10
- **Will all believers suffer and be glorified together with Christ?**
  ○ Verses 17, 30; 2Tim 2:12
- Read Mark 13:13. **What consequences will face Christians who do not endure unto the end?**
  ○ 2Tim 2:11–13; Mark 13:13; Jas 1:12; Col 1:21–23; verse 25

19–22 "creature", "creation"
- **What is the "creature"?**
- **Is the "creature" of verses 19–21 the same as the "creation" of verse 22?**
- **Why are the creature and the creation personified in verses 19–22?**
- **In what way does the creation "groaneth and travaileth in pain"?**
- **Why does Paul discuss the creation?**

"subject to vanity", "bondage of corruption"
- **What does "subject to vanity" mean?**
- **In what way was the creature made subject to vanity under the bondage to corruption?**
  ○ Gen 3:17–18

23 "which have the firstfruits of the Spirit"
- **What are "firstfruits"?**

- Ex 23:19; Deut 26:10; Eze 44:30
- **In verse 23, does "firstfruits of the Spirit" mean that the Spirit is the firstfruits or that the firstfruits come from the Spirit?**
- 1Cor 15:20–24; Jas 1:18

"we ourselves groan within ourselves"

- **What does it mean for us to groan "within ourselves"?**
- Verse 26

"waiting for the adoption"

- We read in verse 16 that we "*are* the children of God" and in verse 15 that we "*have received* the Spirit of adoption". Yet verse 23 indicates we are "waiting" for the adoption. **Are Christians not yet sons of God?**

"the redemption of our body"

- **Will the bodies of all believers in Christ be redeemed?**
- **Why does Paul write "body" (singular) and not "bodies" (plural)?**

24–25 "what a man seeth, why doth he yet hope for?"

- **By his question in verse 24, does Paul imply that there is no evidence for an afterlife?**

26 "Likewise the Spirit also helpeth our infirmities"

- **To what does the Spirit help our infirmities likewise?**
- Verse 22
- **What are these infirmities?**

"we know not what we should pray for as we ought"

- **Why don't we know for what we should pray? Didn't Jesus teach us how to pray?**
- Matt 6:9–13; Eph 6:18; Jude 20
- **Is the Lord's Prayer (see Matt 6:9–13) a prayer that we should repeat verbatim or does it only provide a general outline into which we should substitute our specific needs?**
- **Does repetition of traditional prayers or creeds please God?**
- Matt 6:7

27 "he that searcheth the hearts"

- **In verse 27, does "he" refer to the Father, the Son, the Holy Spirit, or someone else?**

28 "all things work together for good"
- How can all things work together for good to us when we don't live in a paradise?
- Does God cause all things to work for good or do they work for good without His intervention?
- How can destructive, hurtful, or traumatic situations work for good?
- Recall Paul's statement that "we glory in tribulations" (Rom 5:3). Can you think of any tribulations in your life that worked out for your good? Have some not?

"to them that love God"
- Who are them "that love God"?
- Can someone love God and not be a Christian?
- Can someone be a Christian and not love God?
  - 1John 5:1–3; John 2:15, 23; 5:22–23; 10:30; 8:19, 42; 15:23; Luke 10:16
- How do we love God?
  - Matt 22:37–39; 25:34–40; Mark 12:28–31
- Jesus said "thou shalt love the Lord thy God with all thy heart, and with all thy soul, and with all thy mind, and with all thy strength" (Mark 12:30). How can we do this? Specifically:
  - What does it mean to love the Lord "with all your heart"?
  - What does it mean to love the Lord "with all your soul"?
  - What does it mean to love the Lord "with all your mind"?
  - What does it mean to love the Lord "with all your strength"?

29–30 "foreknow", "predestinate", "called"
- When and in what way did God foreknow people?
- What does it mean for God to "predestinate" people to be conformed to the image of his Son?
- How are people called?
  - 1Pe 1:1–2, 20–21; Mark 13:19–20; Col 3:12; Eph 1:3–12
- Are only Christians "called"?
- Is it possible for people to reject the call of God?
- Does God's foreknowledge effectively mean that we have no free will?

- Do people have any choice about or influence over whether they are saved?
  - Luke 13:3, 5; Acts 3:19; Eze 18:23, 27, 32. 2Cor 7:9–10.

"predestinate to be conformed to the image of his Son"
- What does being "conformed to the image of his Son" entail?
  - 2Cor 3:15–18; Col 1:15; Heb 1:3
- Read Gen 1:26–27. What are the differences between being created "in the image of God" (Gen 1:27) and being "conformed to the image of his Son"?
  - 1Cor 11:7; 15:42–49
- God has often foretold the future through His prophets. How does He do this? Is He able to predict the future actions and interactions of independent actors or does He just cause events to happen in the way that He has indicated they will?

31–37 "If God be for us, who can be against us?"
- By his second question in verse 31, does Paul imply that we should be able to overcome all obstacles easily since none can withstand God's will?

"delivered him up for us all"
- Did Christ die for everyone in the world or for only the elect of verse 33?
- Would it be appropriate for a person today to deliver up his child if it could help a larger community?
  - Gen 22:1–10; 19:1–8; Jdg 19:16–25

"Who shall lay any thing to the charge of God's elect?", "Who is he that condemneth?"
- In verses 33 and 34, Paul seems to imply that no one can lay anything to the charge of God's elect and that no one will condemn us. How does this relate to the constant accusations of the accuser of Rev 12:10?
  - Verse 1
    - Aside: Who is the accuser of Rev 12:10?
- Who will lay things to the charge of those who are *not* God's elect?
- Who will condemn non-Christians?

"in all these things we are more than conquerors"
- Who or what do Christians conquer?

38–39 "For I am persuaded"
- Why does Paul start the sentence of verses 38–39 with "For I am persuaded" instead of just asserting that "Neither death, nor life, nor ... shall be able to separate us from the love of God"? Doesn't this phrase weaken his statement?
  ○ Luke 1:1
    - Aside: In some of his writings (such as 1Cor 7:12, 25), Paul states that he is not speaking from the Lord on specific issues. **On such issues, should we consider Paul's opinion to be Scripture?**
      - **If not, then does this suggest that not all parts of the Bible are inspired by God?**
      - **If so, then how can we consider such passages to be inspired by God when Paul himself stated that it was not from the Lord?**

"... nor any other creature, shall be able to separate us from the love of God"
- Who is "us" in verse 39?
  ○ Rom 7:4; 5:8
- Why are angels, principalities, powers, and every other creature powerless to separate us from the love of God?
  ○ 1Pe 3:22
- Why are angels included in this list of things that cannot separate us from the love of God? Would angels want to separate us from that love?

Romans 9

1–2 "I say the truth in Christ"
- **Why does Paul add "in Christ" to the statement "I say the truth" in verse 1?**
  - Rom 8:16; 1John 5:9–12; John 5:32; 2Cor 11:10

"my conscience also bearing me witness in the Holy Ghost"
- **How does Paul's conscience bear him witness "in the Holy Ghost"?**

"I have great heaviness and continual sorrow in my heart"
- **Why was Paul sad?**

3 "I could wish that myself were accursed from Christ"
- **What does "accursed" mean?**
  - Matt 25:41,46; Gal 3:10–14; verse 3
- **Does Paul really wish he were accursed for this brethren? How could Paul be willing to sever his relationship with Christ under any circumstances?**
- We might be willing to lose the lives in our temporary bodies for someone. **Could or should we be willing to lose eternal life for another person?**

4–5 "the fathers"
- **Who are the fathers?**
  - Ex 3:6; Acts 3:13; 7:8

"to whom pertaineth the adoption, and the glory, ... and the promises"
- **Is there any order to this list of items in verse 4 that pertain to the Israelites?**

"the covenants"
- **What is a covenant?**
- **How many covenants did God make with the Israelites?**

- **Do all covenants with God have a similar structure?**

"God blessed for ever"
- **What does the phrase "God blessed for ever" mean?**

"Amen"
- **Why did Paul write "Amen" at the end of verse 5?**

6–9 "Not as though the word of God hath taken none effect"
- **What would it mean for the word of God to have "taken none effect"?**
  ○ Gen 17:1–14, 21. Lev 26:14–16, 40–45. Jer 31:31–34; Rom 11:26–29.
- Read Gen 17:1–14. **How is the covenant between God and Abraham related to the new covenant mentioned in Heb 12:24?**
  ○ Rom 2:25–29; 4:11
- **Is a covenant the same as a testament (see Luke 22:20)? If not, then what are the differences?**
- In Rom 11:1–2, Paul states clearly that God has not rejected His people. **Should fulfillment of the promise to the Israelites be important to Christians?**
  - **If so, then why is it important?**
  - **If not, then why does Paul write about the Israelites to the Romans?**

"they are not all Israel, which are of Israel"
- In Rom 2:28–29 Paul makes statements similar to those in verses 6–8. **Is there a difference between the terms "Israelites" (verse 4) and "Jews"?**

"children of the flesh", "children of God", "children of the promise"
- **Who are the "children of the flesh" of the Old Testament?**
- **Who are the "children of the promise" of the Old Testament?**
  ○ Gen 16:1–4; 17:15–21; 21:1–3, 12
- **Who are the "children of flesh" of the New Testament?**
- **Who are the "children of promise" of the New Testament?**
  ○ Gal 4:22–31; 3:29
- **Does God regard Jews differently than Gentiles now that Christ has come?**

"counted for the seed"

Romans 9

- What does "counted for the seed" mean in verse 8?
- Are the children of the promise of the Old Testament regarded as heirs with the children of promise of the New Testament?
    - If not, then what will they receive given the unfailing promises of God?
    - If so, then will even such children who do not turn to Christ be saved?
  ○ Rom 11:25–29; Isa 59:20

10–13 "Rebecca also"
- What do Sarah and Rebecca have in common?
- What does this common attribute represent?
- Were Esau and Jacob both children of promise like Isaac?

"had conceived by one"
- Why does Paul add "by one" in verse 10?

"not of works, but of him that calleth"
- What does verse 11 mean?
  ○ Eph 2:8–9

"the elder shall serve the younger"
- When did Esau serve Jacob?

"Jacob", "Esau"
- How do Jacob and Esau relate to us today?
  ○ Heb 11:20; 12:15–17; Mal 1:2–3; Gen 25:27; 26:34–35

"Jacob have I loved, but Esau have I hated"
- Does God love some people but hate others? Does He love some people more than others?
    - If not, then how can we explain God's special relationship with the nation of Israel?
    - If so, then does this seem unfair?
    ○ Verses 20–21
  ○ Luke 14:26; Matt 10:37–38; John 3:16; 1Tim 2:3–6. Rom 1:7; John 20:2.

14–16 "it is not of him that willeth, nor of him that runneth"
- What is "it"? That is, what is not of him that willeth nor of him that runneth?
- What would the man who wills want?
- Where would the man who runs go?
  ○ Verse 11

17–21 "for this same purpose", "whom he will he hardeneth"
- In Ex 10:1, the Lord states "I have hardened (Pharaoh's) heart". **Why did God harden Pharaoh's heart?**
  ◦ Ex 9:12–16; verse 22

"Why doth he yet find fault?"
- **Do the questions of verse 19 seem reasonable?**
  ◦ Isa 45:9–10
- **What is wrong with the argument that if God hardens some (see also Rom 11:7–8), then He should not find fault with them?**

"O man, who art thou"
- **Is the response in verse 20 satisfying?**

22–24 "to make his power known, endured with much longsuffering the vessels of wrath fitted for destruction"
- **Was destruction the unavoidable end for which the vessels of wrath of verse 22 were fitted?**
  - **If not, then how should we interpret the phrase "fitted for destruction"?**
  - **If so, then who fitted them for destruction?**
    - **If God, then for why would He endure them if they were to be destroyed?**
    - **If not God, then who and how?**
- **Does the idea that certain vessels are fitted for destruction imply that some people are created for the lake of fire and have no chance at eternal life?**
  ◦ Rom 5:18; Eze 18:30–32; Matt 18:14; 1Tim 2:3–4; 2Pe 3:9

"that he might make known the riches of his glory on the vessels of mercy"
- **How does God's endurance of vessels of wrath make known the riches of his glory on vessels of mercy?**

25–29 "I will call them my people, which were not my people"
- **How did Jews regard Gentiles formerly?**
  ◦ Acts 10:9–17, 34–35, 44–48; 11:8; Matt 10:5–6

"For he will finish the work, and cut it short in righteousness", "a short work will the Lord make upon the earth"
- **What is the work of verse 28?**
- **What does it mean for the Lord to "cut it short in righteousness"?**

"seed"

- What is the "seed" in verse 29?

"we had been as Sodom"
- Does the sentence "we had been as Sodom" mean:
  (a) They would have been like Sodom if the Lord had not left them a seed?
  (b) They were like Sodom until the Lord left them a seed?
  (c) Something else?
- Does the statement by Isaiah in verse 29 suggest that God might have totally destroyed Israel under some circumstance?

30–33 "Gentiles, which followed not after righteousness"
- Does verse 30 indicate that the Gentiles did not try to be righteous?

"stumblingstone"
- What is the "stumblingstone" of verses 32–33?
- In what way did Israel stumble over this stone?
  ◦ 1Pet 2:8; Matt 21:42–44; Isa 8:13–15; 1Cor 1:22–24; Rom 11:11

Romans 10

1–5 "Brethren"
- Who are the "brethren" of verse 1?
  ◦ Rom 7:1, 4; 8:12; 9:3
- Why does Paul refer to them as "brethren"?
  ◦ Rom 8:14, 29

"they have a zeal of God, but not according to knowledge"
- Is a zeal *of* God the same as a zeal *for* God?
- What signs indicate that a person has a zeal of God?
- Who are "they" of verse 2? Did all the Israelites have a zeal of God?
- To what kind of knowledge was their zeal not according?
  ◦ Verse 3
- Do all Christians have a zeal of God?
- Verses 1 and 2 indicate that zeal of God is insufficient for salvation. Without Christ, is such zeal profitable in any way?

"being ignorant of God's righteousness"
- Did the people of verses 1–3 not believe that God was righteous?
  ◦ Rom 3:21–22; 1:16–17; verse 4; 2Pe 1:1

"going about to establish their own righteousness"
- How did these people try to establish their own righteousness?
  ◦ Eph 2:8–9

"Christ is the end of the law for righteousness"
- Do verse 4 and Rom 6:14 contradict Rom 3:31?

"the man which doeth those things shall live by them"
- Does verse 5 suggest that we can earn eternal life by following the law?

6–10 "Who shall ascend into heaven?", "Who shall descend into the deep?"
- **What do verses 6 and 7 mean?**
- ○ Deut 30:11–14; Eph 4:8–10

"The word is nigh thee"
- **How does the righteousness which is of faith "speak" (verse 6) about the nearness of the word (verse 8)?**

"confess with thy mouth", "believe in thine heart", "unto righteousness", "unto salvation"
- **Does verse 10 indicate that salvation is a two-step process, requiring first belief and second confession? Is belief inadequate without verbal confession?**
- ○ Rom 5:9; Luke 12:8–9; 1John 4:15. John 3:16, 36; 6:40; Acts 16:31.
- **Why does Paul reverse the order of "confess" and "believe" from verse 9 to verse 10? Should not belief always come before confession?**
- Read John 12:42–43. Verse 42 indicates that these rulers believed in Christ, but did not confess Him. **Were these rulers saved?**

11 "Whosoever believeth on him shall not be ashamed"
- **What kind of shame will believers on the Lord Jesus not suffer? Will non-believers suffer this shame?**

12–15 "there is no difference between the Jew the and Greek"
- **Does verse 12 imply that ethnic Jews no longer have special favor with God?**
- ○ Gal 3:28–29

"is rich unto all that call upon him"
- **To what kind of riches does Paul refer in verse 12?**
- ○ Rom 11:12; 9:23; 2Cor 8:9; Eph 2:4, 7; 3:8

"call upon the name of the Lord"
- **How do we call upon the name of the Lord? Is calling upon *the name* of the Lord different from calling upon *the Lord*?**
- ○ Verse 12, 14; Joel 2:28–32; Zep 3:9; Zec 13:9; 1Chr 16:7–8; Gen 12:7–8; Ps 116:12–13

"How then shall they ... ?"
- **What is the purpose of the questions in verses 14–15?**

"how shall they preach, except they be sent?"

- **Who sends the preachers?**
  - Matt 9:37–38

16–21 "But they have not all obeyed the gospel", "Have they not heard?"
- **Who are "they" that did not all obey the gospel?**
  - Rom 1:19–20
- **How could Isaiah speak about the gospel if he lived and died before Christ came?**

"their sound went into all the earth"
- **What is the sound of verse 18?**
- **Whose are the sound and words?**
  - Ps 19:1–4
- **Does verse 18 indicate that everyone has heard the gospel of Christ already?**
  - Rom 16:26

"Did not Israel know?"
- **What might Israel claim that it did not know?**
- **What objection to the idea of salvation through Christ does the question in verse 19 raise?**
- **How can Paul imply in verse 19 that Israel did know, but in verse 3 that they were ignorant?**

"Isaiah is very bold"
- **In what way was Isaiah very bold?**
  - Isa 65:1

Romans 11

1–2 "his people which he foreknew"
- **Who are the people which God foreknew? Are these people the same as those "whom he did foreknow" of Rom 8:29?**

"Israel"
- **Is God's relationship to Israel relevant to Christians? If so, then why?**

3–6 "seven thousand men, who have not bowed the knee to the image of Baal", "according to the election of grace"
- **Was the remnant of verse 4 spared by works (not bowing the knee to Baal) or by grace?**
  - Verses 5–6; 1Ki 19:9–18
    - Aside: In 1Ki 19:9–18, we read that the LORD came to Elijah not in the wind, nor in the earthquake, nor in the fire, but in a still small voice. **What does this tell us about Him?**

"grace"
- Elsewhere (see Rom 3:28; 5:15–17; 6:23; Eph 2:8–9) Paul states that salvation is not based on works of the law nor earned on our own merits, but is granted through the unmerited favor of God. **If salvation comes by the grace of God alone, then are we responsible for our own salvation in any way?**
- Read Acts 16:31. **Is the act of believing a work of ours by which we are saved?**

7–10 "God hath given them the spirit of slumber"
- **Does God continue to give some people a "spirit of slumber"? Do all people who reject Christ do so because God has hardened their hearts?**

- Matt 13:14–17

"Let their table be made a snare"
- **What does it mean for a table to be made a snare?**
  - John 6:32–35

"and bow down their back alway"
- **How would the ones who were hardened "bow down their back"?**
- **Does verse 10 suggest that Israel will be hardened forever, seemingly in contrast to verses 25–26?**

11–15 "salvation is come unto the Gentiles, for to provoke them to jealousy"
- **Did salvation came to the Gentiles only to make the Jews jealous ?**
  - **If so (that is, if God's ultimate plan was the salvation of Israel), then why did He harden them (see verses 7–8)?**
  - **If not (that is, if God's ultimate plan was the salvation of the entire world), then why does Paul speak of the opportunity given the Gentiles in the context of Israel (namely to make the Israelites jealous and to bring about *their* salvation)?**
  - Gal 3:14; 1Tim 2:3–4

"Have they stumbled that they should fall?"
- **What does stumbling and falling mean in verse 11?**

"casting away of them", "receiving of them"
- In verse 1, Paul suggests that God has not cast away his people. In verse 15, he implies that they have been cast away. **How do these verses reconcile?**

16–24 "firstfruit", "lump", "root", "branches"
- **What do the lump and the branches of verse 16 symbolize?**
- **What do the firstfruit and the root of verse 16 symbolize?**
  - Isa 11:1; Num 15:21

"natural branches"
- **Who are the "natural branches" of verse 21?**

"The branches were broken off"
- **Who broke off the branches of verse 17?**
  - Rom 9:6–8; Matt 3:8–10

Romans 11

"a good olive tree"
- **What does "good" mean in the context of verse 24?**
- **How should we interpret the analogy of the tree in verses 16–24?**
- **What special qualities of the olive tree transfer readily to this analogy?**
- Symbolism involving "branches" occurs in other places in Scripture as well. **How does the passage in verses 16–24 relate to John 15:1–6?**

"thou also shalt be cut off"
- **What happens to a person who is "cut off"?**

25-32 "this mystery"
- **What is the mystery that Paul mentions in verse 25?**
  ○ Mark 4:11; 1Cor 2:7; 4:1; Rom 16:25; Eph 3:1–7; Col 2:2

"lest ye should be wise in your own conceits"
- In Rom 12:3 Paul again exhorts each reader "not to think of himself more highly than he ought to think". **Why might the brethren consider themselves wise?**
- **What attitude should a believer have, given that salvation is by grace and not by works?**
  ○ 1Cor 8:1–3; Gal 6:3

"until the fulness of the Gentiles be come in"
- **What is the "fulness of the Gentiles"?**
- **When will the fulness of the Gentiles come in?**

"all Israel will be saved"
- **Does verse 26 contradict Rom 9:27 (that only a remnant of Israel will be saved) or Rom 4:16 (that faith is necessary for salvation) or John 14:6 (that the only way to the Father is by the Son)?**

"the Deliverer ... shall turn away ungodliness from Jacob"
- In Isa 59:20, we read that "the Redeemer shall come to Zion, and unto them that turn from transgression in Jacob". **Does this indicate that the Redeemer will come not to everyone in Jacob, but only to those in Jacob who repent?**
  - **If so, then how will *all* Israel be saved (verse 26)?**
  - **If not, then will repentance not be required of all who are redeemed?**

"the gifts and calling of God are without repentance"
- **Does the statement that the gifts and calling of God**

are without repentance have meaning for Christians?
"God hath concluded them all in unbelief"
- **When did Gentiles not believe?**
- **When did Jews not believe?**
- **Is the unbelief of the Gentiles of the same kind as the unbelief of the Jews?**

33–36 "who hath known the mind of the Lord?"
- **How do verses 33–36 relate to verse 32 and the preceding passage?**

"of him", "through him", "to him"
- **In verse 36, does "him" refer to the Father, the Son, the Holy Spirit, or someone else?**
   ◦ 1Cor 8:6; Col 1:16; Heb 1:2; 2:10; John 1:3
- **In what way are all things of Him?**
- **In what way are all things through Him?**
- **In what way are all things to Him?**
    - **Aside: Does Paul imply in 1Cor 8:6 that Jesus is Lord, but not God?**

Romans 12

1–2 "therefore"
- **According to Paul, why should we present our bodies a living sacrifice?**
  - Rom 11:20–22

"by the mercies of God"
- **What are the "mercies of God"?**
- **How are the mercies of God related to the way that we present our bodies?**
  - Rom 1:5; 1Cor 15:9–10; 2Cor 1:12; Gal 1:15; Eph 3:8

"present your bodies a living sacrifice"
- **What is a "living sacrifice"?**
  - Gen 22:8–12; Heb 9:11–14
    - **Aside: Read Gen 22:8–12. Of who does Isaac serve as a figure?**
      - Heb 11:17–19
- **How do we present our bodies a living sacrifice?**
  - Rom 6:12–13; 1Cor 6:15, 18–20
- **Given Jesus' sacrifice on our behalf, why is additional sacrifice necessary?**

"acceptable unto God"
- In Isa 64:6, we read that "all our righteousnesses are as filthy rags". **Can anything we do be acceptable unto God?**

"which is your reasonable service"
- **Is the presentation of their bodies as a living sacrifice the only service that Christians need to perform?**
- In the Old Testament, the priests presented the sacrifices. **Is Paul likening believers to priests in verse 1?**
  - Rev 1:4–6; 1Pe 2:4–5, 9–10. Heb 7:26–27; 10:10–14.

"be ye transformed by the renewing of your mind"
- **From what and into what are we to be transformed?**

- Php 3:20–21; 2Cor 3:18
- What does it mean for a mind to be renewed?
- How can we renew our mind?
- How does the renewing of our mind transform us?
- How long is this transformative process?
- 2Cor 4:16; Titus 3:5
- Read Php 3:21. Will the individual bodies of all Christians be changed into the kind of glorious body that Christ had?
- Rom 8:29; Matt 7:18

"that ye may prove what is that good, and acceptable, and perfect will of God"

- How do we prove by our transformation what is the will of God?
- By whose standards is the will of God "good"?
- What does "perfect" mean here?
- To whom is God's will "acceptable"?

"brethren", "your bodies", "living sacrifice", "your mind"

- Although Paul is writing to his "brethren" and writes of their "bodies" in the plural tense, he uses the singular tense in referring to "a living and holy sacrifice" and their "mind". Other examples appear in Rom 3:13; 8:23; Eph 4:23; Php 4:23. Is this significant?
- Rom 15:6; 2Cor 13:11; verse 5

3-5 "I say, through the grace given unto me"
- How is Paul's statement of verse 3 made through the grace given unto him?

"but to think soberly, according as God hath dealt to every man the measure of faith"

- What does it mean to "think soberly"?
- How is a sober manner of thinking related to a measure of faith?
- If God deals out faith, then are we responsible for the measure of faith we have?
    - If not, then are non-believers responsible for their lack of faith and its consequences?
    - If so, then:
        - How does our responsibility reconcile with the idea that God deals to us our measure of faith?
        - How can we obtain a greater measure of faith?

"For …"
- How do verses 2, 3, and 4 relate to each other?

"all members have not the same office"
- What are the offices to which verse 4 refers?
- Is there a difference between the statement "all members have not the same office" and the statement "not all members have the same office"?
  ◦ 1Cor 12:12–27

"one body in Christ"
- Read 1Cor 12:27. Is being one body *in* Christ the same as being the body *of* Christ?
  ◦ Eph 4:11–13

"every one members one of another"
- How are Christians "members one of another"?

6–8 "gifts differing according to the grace that is given to us"
- 1Cor 12:31 seems to indicate that some gifts are greater then others. Has each one of us been given a different amount of grace, where people with greater gifts have been given greater grace?
- Is it possible to receive more grace?
  - If not, then how is the amount of grace given to us determined?
  - If so, then what can we do to get it?
  ◦ Rom 5:1–2; 1Cor 12:31

"whether prophecy, let us prophecy according to the proportion of faith"
- Is one's ability to prophesy proportional to the size of one's faith?
  ◦ 1Cor 12:28–29; 14:1–5, 37

"prophecy", "ministry", "teacheth", "exhorteth", "giveth", "ruleth", "showeth mercy"
- What is "exhortation"?
- Are the seven gifts in verses 6–8 listed in any kind of order?
  ◦ 1Cor 12:28; Eph 4:11–12

"ruleth"
- What are the duties of one who rules? Is such a ruler part of the government?
- Is the ruler of verse 8 of the same kind as the ruler of Rom 13:1–7?

9 "Let love be without dissimulation"
- **What is "dissimulation"?**
- **How would love *with* dissimulation manifest itself?**

"Abhor that which is evil; cleave to that which is good"
- Read Mark 7:20–23. **Should we feel repugnance toward all those evil things which "come from within"?**
- **Does the world deaden our abhorrence of sin?**
- **How should we react when we see evil things proceeding from others?**
- We are told to "cleave" to what is good. **Is something trying to pull us away from what is good?**
- 1Th 5:21–22; Amos 5:15

10–13 "in honor preferring one another"
- **How might we prefer one another in honor?**
- Luke 14:8

"serving the Lord"
- **How do we serve the Lord, since He has no need for anything from us?**
- Verse 1; Matt 25:34–40; Mark 10:42–45; Luke 2:37; 22:26–27

14–16 "Bless them which persecute you"
- **Is it possible for us to bless sincerely those who persecute us?**
- Verse 20; Matt 5:10, 43–45

"Rejoice with them that do rejoice, and weep with them that weep"
- **Why should people rejoice with them that rejoice and weep with them that weep?**

17–21 "Recompense to no man evil for evil"
- **Should we allow others to do evil to us without consequence?**

"Provide things honest in the sight of all men."
- **What does it mean to "provide things honest"?**
- **Is it fine to provide things dishonest when out of the sight of men?**

"If it be possible ... live peaceably with all men"
- **Will it sometimes not be possible to live peaceably with all men?**

"in so doing thou shalt heap coals of fire on his head"
- Read Pr 25:21–22. **Would it be wrong for us to do good to our enemies with the motive of heaping coals of fire upon their heads?**

"Be not overcome of evil, but overcome evil with good"
- **How can one be overcome of evil?**
- **How can one overcome evil with good?**

Romans 13

1–2 "Let every soul be subject unto the higher powers"
- **Who are the higher powers of verse 1? Are they officials in government? Leaders in church? Supervisors at work? Bullies at school?**
- **Was the American Revolution wrong?**
- **Should we obey our leaders even if they tell us to do something immoral?**
  ○ Dan 3 (Shadrach, Meshach, Abednego); Acts 5:29

"the powers that be are ordained of God"
- **Were such leaders as Hitler, Stalin, and Pol Pot placed in power by God?**
  ○ Matt 2:3
- **Were the atrocities committed under the regimes of these people part of God's plan?**

"Whosoever therefore resisteth the power, resisteth the ordinance of God"
- **Must we obey every law and rule set by authorities?**
- **Is there ever an appropriate time to resist authority?**
  ○ Acts 5:27–29, 40–42
- **Is it wrong to vote against an incumbent in a democracy?**
- **Is it wrong to distribute Bibles illegally in countries hostile to Christianity?**

3–7 "For rulers are not a terror to good works"
- Read Acts 16:22–24. Paul suffered persecution and imprisonment at the hands of authorities for spreading the good news of Jesus Christ. **How can he say in verse 3 that rulers will give praise to those who do good and that they are not a terror to good works?**

"for he beareth not the sword in vain; for he is the minister

of God"
- Why does Paul write *the* power (verse 3) and *the* minister (verse 4) instead of *a* power and *a* minister? Does not more than one ruler hold power? If not, then who is this particular ruler?
- What does "minister of God" mean in verse 4? Is a ruler a pastor?

"not only for wrath"
- Does "wrath" in verse 5 refer to the wrath of God or the wrath of human rulers?
- Given that all authority is from God (verse 1), is the wrath of human rulers a form of the wrath of God?

"for they are God's ministers"
- Are all rulers ministers of God?
  - If so, then in what way do evil rulers serve God?
  - If not, then why doesn't Paul indicate that there are exceptions?

"attending continually upon this very thing"
- What is this "very thing" of verse 6 upon which rulers attend continually?

"tribute"
- Is it wrong to evade taxes?
- Is it wrong to transact business in the "black market" in violation of governmental regulations?
  ○ Matt 22:15–21

8–10 "Owe no man anything"
- Should Christians ever borrow money?
- Should Christians lend money at interest?
  ○ Deut 15:6, 23:19–20; Lev 25:37

"he that loveth another hath fulfilled the law", "love is the fulfilling of the law"
- Can we love others without knowing Christ?
  ○ Gal 5:14; Luke 10:25–27; Matt 22:36–40; Luke 6:31.
  - If so, then if by loving others we can fulfill the law (verse 8), why did Christ need to come?
  - If not, then what does Christ do for us that allows us to love others?
  ○ Rom 8:3–4; Matt 5:17–18. Matt 22:36–40.
- Paul writes in Rom 3:28 that "a man is justified by faith" and mentions in 2Tim 3:15 the "salvation through faith

which is in Christ Jesus". He also writes in 1Cor 13:13 that "the greatest of (faith, hope, charity) is charity". **If charity is greater than faith, then can we be saved through charity without having faith?**
- If so, then is belief in Christ not necessary for salvation?
- If not, then in what sense is charity greater than faith?
- Aside: What does it mean for faith, hope, charity to "abide", as written in 1Cor 13:13?
- What is "charity"? Is charity the same as love?

11–14 "it is high time to awake out of sleep"
- Who is asleep in verse 11?
- What does Paul mean by "awake out of sleep"? Does not one have to be awake to be reading those words?

"night", "day"
- To what do "night" and "day" refer in verse 12?
  ○ 1Th 5:4–8; Rev 21:22–27

"for now is our salvation nearer than when we believed"
- In what sense was salvation nearer now than before?
- Was Paul suggesting by the phrase "than when we believed" that he no longer believed?
  - If not, then when did he believe?
  - If so, then how does this statement of lack of faith reconcile with Paul's testimony in the rest of Romans and his other letters?

"put on the armor of light", "put ye on the Lord Jesus Christ"
- What is the "armor of light"?
- What does this armor protect against?
- How does one "put on" the armor of light and the Lord Jesus Christ?

Romans 14

1–4 "but not to doubtful disputations"
- **What does "not to doubtful disputations" mean?**
"another, who is weak, eateth herbs"
- **Does "weak" mean physically weak here?**
- Verse 1
- **Does verse 2 imply that people who are weak eat only herbs or that people who eat only herbs are weak?**
  - **If the former, then are people who eat meat always strong?**
  - **If the latter, then are no strong people vegetarians?**
"another man's servant", "to his own master", "for God is able to make him stand"
- **Does verse 4 imply that he who eats serves a master other than Christ?**
  - **If not, then to whom do "another man" and "his own master" refer?**
  - **If so, then:**
    - **Why would God make him stand?**
    - **Who is the other master?**

5–6 "Let every man be fully persuaded in his own mind"
- In Ex 20:8, God commanded the Israelites to "remember the sabbath day, to keep it holy". **Does Paul imply in verse 5 that remembering the sabbath day is no longer important?**

7–9 "For none of us liveth to himself, and no man dieth to himself"
- **Does the inclusion of the phrase "of us" in the first clause of verse 7 imply any contrast with the second?**
- Luke 20:38

"we die unto the Lord"
- **In verse 8, does dying "unto the Lord" refer to martyrdom?**

"whether we live therefore, or die"
- **What was Paul's attitude toward death?**
  - Php 1:18–26
    - Aside: In Php 1:21–22, Paul states that he does not know what to choose: to live or to die. **Why would he even consider choosing between life and death? Is it appropriate for anyone to grant himself this choice?**
    - **What does the Bible teach about suicide?**
    - Ex 20:13

"Lord both of the dead and living"
- **Can people who died before the death and resurrection of Christ gain eternal life?**
  - 1Pe 4:5–6; 3:18–20
- **How does verse 9 reconcile with Mark 12:27, in which Jesus says that God "is not the God of the dead"?**
  - Mark 12:26
    - Aside: Read Mark 12:26–27. **Do these verses suggest that Abraham, Isaac, and Jacob are living and not dead? If so, then how was this possible?**
    - Gen 25:8; 35:29; 49:33

10–13 "why dost thou judge thy brother", "Let us not therefore judge one another"
- **How do verses 10 and 13 reconcile with the implication of 1Cor 5:12 that we are to judge those within the church?**
  - 1Cor 5:3

"we shall all stand before the judgment seat of Christ", "every one of us shall give account of himself to God"
- **Who will judge us: the Father or the Son?**
  - John 5:22; 2Cor 5:10
- **Will the day of judgment be a fearful or a joyful time for Christians?**
- **What kind of judgment should Christians expect?**
- **Will God punish the Christian and the non-Christian in the same way for equivalent sins?**
  - **If not, then:**

Romans 14

- What is the difference in punishments?
- Is it fair that the punishments will be different?
- Is so, then why should anyone care to place faith in Christ?
- For which of the following will we be held accountable?
  (a) our actions
  (b) our words
  (c) our thoughts
  (d) our temptations
  ○ Matt 16:27; 12:36; Heb 4:12, 15

14-18 "there is nothing unclean of itself"
- **Does Paul imply in verses 5 and 14 that sin is subjective and that a person who is convinced of the rectitude of his actions violates no absolute standards of morality?**
○ Verse 23; Pr 16:25; 1Cor 6:9–10
- **If Paul knows that nothing is unclean in itself, then should we also consider all things to be clean?**
- **If all meat is clean and if vegetarianism comes from weak faith (verse 2), then why should anyone consider vegetarianism?**
○ 1Cor 10:25–26

"but to him that esteemeth any thing to be unclean, to him it is unclean"
- **Does Paul suggest in verse 14 that given two identical acts performed under similar circumstances, one may be considered sin and the other not sin?**
○ Verse 22–23

"Destroy not him with thy meat, for whom Christ died"
- **How could people destroy him who is saved through Christ?**

"Let not then your good be evil spoken of"
- Suppose a believer who was a vegetarian were to demand that you not eat meat. **How would you respond?**
  - If you were to continue eating meat, then would not this response cause him to stumble (verse 21)?
  - If you were to stop eating meat, then:
    - Would you not be allowing this good thing to "be evil spoken of" (verse 16)?

71

- Would you be implicitly testifying that you believe some things are unclean?
  - Verses 14, 21

"the kingdom of God is ... righteousness, and peace, and joy in the Holy Ghost"

- **Does verse 17 define the kingdom of God or merely describe life in the kingdom?**
  - **If it defines the kingdom, then why isn't God the Father mentioned within the definition of His own kingdom?**
  - **If it only describes life there, then what exactly is the "kingdom of God"?**
- **Is the "kingdom of God" the same as the "kingdom of heaven"?**
  - Matt 5:3; 10:7; 13:24; 18:1
    - **If so, then why are both phrases used?**
    - **If not, then what is the difference between them?**

"he that in these things serveth Christ is acceptable to God, and approved of men"

- **What are "these things" of verse 18?**

"approved of men"

- **Does serving Christ always gain approval from men?**
- **Should we seek approval from men?**
  - 1Th 1:6–9

19–23 "follow after the things which make for peace, and things wherewith one may edify another"

- **Is war always wrong or is it sometimes justifiable?**

"destroy not the work of God"

- **To what work of God is verse 20 referring?**
  - Verse 15

"to drink wine"

- **Is it wrong to drink wine or alcoholic beverages?**
  - **If so, then:**
    - **How does Paul's assertion in verse 14 that there "is nothing unclean of itself" apply here?**
    - **Why did Jesus turn water into wine (John 2:1–11) if drinking wine was wrong?**
  - **If not, then:**
    - **Is drunkenness also acceptable?**
    - Eph 5:18; Gal 5:21

- **Should we encourage people to drink alcohol?**

"whatsoever is not of faith is sin"
- **What does the statement "whatsoever is not of faith is sin" mean?**

Romans 15

1–3 "We then that are strong ought to bear the infirmities of the weak"
- **How can we bear the infirmities of other people?**
  ○ Verses 3, 7; Rom 14:1; Gal 6:2
"and not to please ourselves"
- **Is it wrong to please ourselves?**
- **Is it wrong to spend money on entertainment when we could give it to the poor?**
  ○ John 12:5–6; Deut 14:26
"Let every one of us please his neighbor for his good"
- **Who is my neighbor?**
  ○ Luke 10:29–37
- **Does Paul imply in verse 2 that we should do whatever our neighbors ask of us?**
"The reproaches of them that reproached thee fell on me"
- **Who reproached whom in verse 3?**
- **When did these reproaches fall upon Christ?**
"even Christ pleased not himself"
- **Whom did Christ please?**
- **If Christ had pleased Himself, then how would He have acted differently?**
- **Do verse 3 and Matt 26:39 suggest that the will of the Son could and did diverge from that of the Father?**
  ○ Matt 26:42; John 10:17–18; Luke 3:22
- **Is there any connection between pleasing God and pleasing our neighbor for his good?**

4–7 "whatsoever things were written aforetime were written for our learning"
- **To which things is Paul referring in verse 4?**
- **How are these things written aforetime instructive to**

us today?
- Gal 3:24; 1Cor 9:9–10

"patience and comfort of the scriptures"
- **Is it important to read the Bible regularly?**
- **What are the consequences of not reading the Bible?**
- **How often and for how long should people read the Bible?**

"likeminded", "with one mind and one mouth"
- **Is the division of the church into multiple denominations contrary to God's will?**
- 1Cor 1:12–13
- **Can theological conflicts between people of different denominations be resolved?**
  - **If so, then how?**
  - **If not, then is such resolution worth pursuing?**

"glorify God"
- **What does it mean to "glorify" God?**
- **How can we glorify God with a single mind and single mouth?**

"receive ye one another, as Christ also received us, to the glory of God"
- **In what way did Christ receive us?**
- **Can our holy God receive sinners?**
- **In receiving us, how was Christ acting to the glory of God?**
- Verses 8–9

8–13 "Jesus Christ was a minister of the circumcision"
- **Who is "the circumcision"?**
- **How was Christ a minister of the circumcision?**
- Matt 20:28
- **Was Christ a minister of the Gentiles also?**

"to confirm the promises made unto the fathers"
- **What promises did Christ confirm as a minister of the circumcision?**

"that the Gentiles might glorify God for his mercy"
- **What is the connection between Christ's ministry to the circumcision and God's mercy to the Gentiles?**
- Verse 10; Eph 2:12

"For this cause I will confess … in him shall the Gentiles trust", "And again"

- Do the four passages in verses 9–12 that Paul quotes from the Old Testament all have the same meaning (with three of them being redundant)?
  ○ 2Sam 22:50; Deut 32:43; Ps 117:1; Isa 11:10

"Now the God of hope fill you with all joy and peace in believing"
- How does God fill us with joy and peace?
  ○ Rom 14:17

14–21 "ye also are full of goodness"
- How can the brethren be full of goodness given both Jesus' statement that "none is good, save one, that is God" (Luke 18:19) and Paul's statement that "in me ... dwelleth no good thing" (Rom 7:18)?

"filled with all knowledge"
- In Pr 28:5 we read that "they that seek the Lord understand all things". What does it mean to be "filled with all knowledge" or to "understand all things"? Does it mean to be omniscient like God?
- If the readers of this letter were filled with all knowledge, then did they have any more to learn?
  ○ 1Cor 8:2; Gen 2:16–17
- Paul states in 1Cor 8:1 that "knowledge puffeth up". If this is the case, then is having knowledge good?
  ○ Ecc 1:18

"able also to admonish one another"
- Paul states "let us not therefore judge one another" in Rom 14:13. How can we admonish one another without being judgmental?

"I have written the more boldly unto you in some sort"
- In what sort has Paul written the more boldly?

"I will not dare to speak of any of those things which Christ hath not wrought by me"
- Is Paul suggesting in verse 18 that every single word he speaks will communicate what Christ wrought by him?
- What did Christ work through Paul?
- Does Christ work anything through us?

"signs and wonders"
- What is a "sign"?
- What is a "wonder"?

- What is the purpose of signs and wonders?
- Read Acts 14:3; 15:12. **What miracles did Christ work through Paul? Which of these miracles were signs and which were wonders?**
  - Acts 13:11; 14:8–10, 19–20; 19:11–12; 20:9–12; 28:1–8
- **Have you witnessed any miracles personally?**

"lest I should build upon another man's foundation"

- **Why would Paul not want to build upon the foundation of another man?**
  - 1Cor 3:10–11
- **Is it wrong for missionaries to go where others have already gone rather than to a place where the natives never heard the gospel?**

"To whom he was not spoken of, they shall see"

- **How does the situation of the people of verse 21 compare with the situation of the Jews?**
  - Matt 13:14; Rom 10:18–19

26–29 "partakers of their spiritual things"

- **How had the Gentiles partaken of the spiritual things of the saints in Jerusalem?**
  - Rom 11:17–18; John 4:22; Col 1:12; Eph 2:12; 3:6; 1Cor 9:11

"When ... I have performed this, and have sealed to them this fruit"

- **What is the "fruit" of verse 28? Are the fruits of verse 28, 1:13, and 6:22 all of the same kind?**
  - Verse 27c; Rom 1:13
- **How will Paul seal this fruit to them?**

"I shall come in the fulness of the blessing of the gospel of Christ"

- **What does it mean for Paul to come "in the fulness of the blessing of the gospel of Christ"?**

30–33 "strive together with me in your prayers"

- **How can we "strive" in prayer? By praying longer or more often? By concentrating harder?**

Romans 16

5 "greet the church that is in their house"
  - The gospel of Christ spread quickly in the early days of the church when believers met for worship in houses. **Can Christians spread the gospel more effectively in small, decentralized congregations than in large, centralized organizations?**
  - Most Christians today meet for worship on Sundays in large (and often fancy) buildings that have been erected for that specific purpose. But it takes a lot of time and money to erect and maintain buildings. **Should Christians today meet for worship in houses instead of such buildings? Why or why not?**
  - **Can controversies over expenditures cause dissension in a church?**
  - **How should a member of a church act if he believes that stewards squander his donations? Should he:**
     (a) withhold his donations in the future?
     (b) seethe inwardly with rage but continue to donate at the same level?
     (c) find a new church?
     (d) raise a big stink?
     (e) conspire to place himself and his allies in positions to disburse the funds?
     (f) other?

16 "Salute one another with a holy kiss"
  - **Would it be appropriate today to salute one another with a holy kiss? Would it make a difference if the other person were exceptionally good looking?**

17–20 "they ... serve ... their own belly"

- Refer to Rom 6:16–22; 7:25. **Is serving one's own belly the same as serving sin?**

"wise unto that which is good, and simple concerning evil"
- **Does the last part of verse 19 simply mean "do good and do no evil"?**
- Matt 10:16; Php 2:15

"the God of peace shall bruise Satan under your feet"
- **When did or will God bruise Satan under their feet?**
- Gen 3:15; Rom 12:19

22 "I Tertius, who wrote this epistle"
- **Why did Tertius write the epistle for Paul (Rom 1:1)?**
- Gal 4:12–15; 6:11; 2Th 3:17; Acts 9:18

25–27 "him that is of power to stablish you"
- **How God establish us?**
- 1Pe 5:10

"revelation of the mystery"
- Paul mentions this mystery not only in verse 25, but also in Rom 11:25. **How was this mystery revealed?**
- Col 2:2–3. Eph 1:9–12; 3:3–6.

"the mystery ... now is ... made known to all nations"
- **Was the mystery known to all nations at the time that Paul wrote the letter?**
  - **If so, then why was there a need for missionaries such as Paul?**
  - **If not, then what is meant here?**
- **Is the mystery known to all nations today?**

"the commandment of the everlasting God"
- **To which commandment of God is Paul referring in verse 26?**

"To God only wise"
- **Do other gods exist, but they are all foolish?**

"through Jesus Christ"
- Paul uses the phrases "through Jesus Christ" or "in Jesus Christ" frequently in his letter to the Romans when he refers to his relationship with the Father. **Why?**
- Rom 1:8; 5:1; 6:11; 7:25; 15:17; John 14:6

Glossary

- accursed -

- apostle -

- baptize -

- blaspheme -

- blessed -

- covenant -

- dissimulation -

- eternal life -

- exhortation -

- faith -

- firstfruits -

- glorify -

- glory -

- gospel -

- grace -

- holy -

- impute -

- justify -

Glossary

- manifest -

- oracles -

- propitiation -

- redemption -

- righteousness -

- saint -

- salvation -

- sanctify -

- seal -

- sign -

- sin -

- type -

- wonder -

- worship -

About the Author

The author was born in North Dakota and resides presently in Oregon.

www.ingramcontent.com/pod-product-compliance
Lightning Source LLC
LaVergne TN
LVHW011733060526
838200LV00051B/3168